Hanukkah 2001

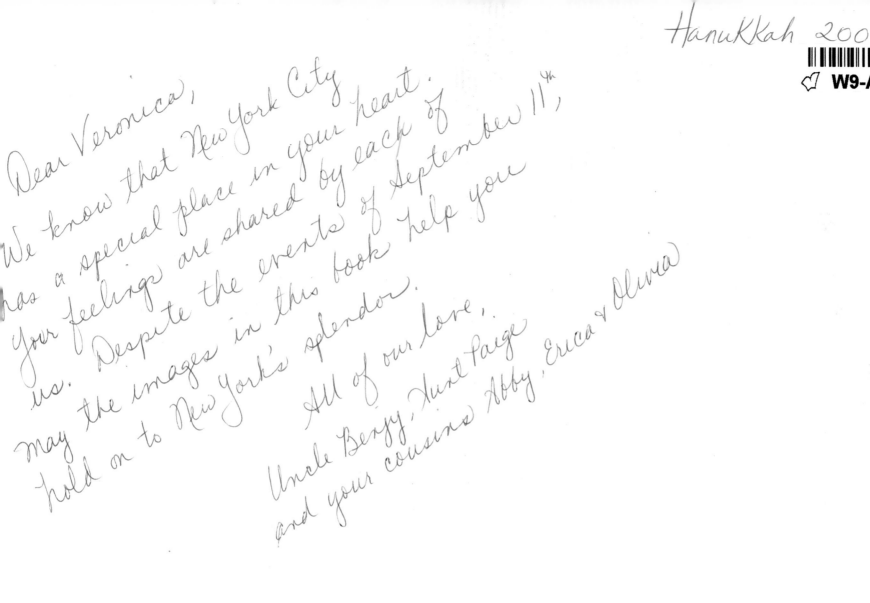

Dear Veronica,

We know that New York City has a special place in your heart. Your feelings are shared by each of us. Despite the events of September 11th, may the images in this book help you hold on to New York's splendor.

All of our love,

Uncle Bergy, Aunt Paige and your cousins Abby, Erica & Olivia

NEW YORK

FROM THE AIR

NEW YORK

FROM THE AIR

JoAnn Padgett

THUNDER BAY
P·R·E·S·S

Published in the United States by
Thunder Bay Press
5880 Oberlin Drive, San Diego, CA 92121-4794
www.advantagebooksonline.com

Produced by PRC Publishing Ltd
Kiln House, 210 New Kings Road
London SW6 4NZ

All notations of errors or omissions should be addressed to Thunder Bay Press,
editorial department, at the above address. All other correspondence (author inquiries,
permissions and rights) concerning the content of this book should be addressed to
PRC Publishing Ltd, Kiln House, 210 New Kings Road, London SW6 4NZ.

ISBN 1-57145-276-1

Library of Congress Cataloging-in-Publication Data available upon request.

Printed and bound in Italy

1 2 3 4 5 00 01 02 03

Front cover
This aerial view shot from New York Bay facing the tip of Battery Park highlights the skyscrapers of
the financial district, with the city's tallest buildings, the 110-story World Trade Center towers,
clearly dominating the skyline. On the left New York Bay curves off to form the Hudson River and
on the right side it becomes the East River (on the south) and the Harlem River (on the north).

page iii
A symbol of freedom throughout the world, the Statue of Liberty is the most enduring image of
New York City. Situated near the center of New York Bay, the gateway to the New World for millions
of immigrants, the Statue of Liberty symbolized not only freedom from political and social oppres-
sion but also America itself. An estimated 12 million people were processed at Ellis Island. Today,
some 40 percent of living Americans can trace their roots to an ancestor who came through Ellis
Island.

ACKNOWLEDGMENTS

All the photography for this book, including the front and back cover photography, was taken by
Simon Clay, with the exception of the following:

Page 131 courtesy of © Joseph Sohm; ChromoSohm Inc./CORBIS;
Page 140-141 courtesy of © Jim Zuckerman/CORBIS;
Page 142-143 courtesy of © Tom Bean/CORBIS.

To my exceptional parents, for the love, laughter, support,
encouragement, happy home, and four wonderful sisters they gave me.
And to Ken and Kelly, who tolerated hours of neglect during the writing
of this book, and who are greatly loved.

INTRODUCTION

Before the arrival of European explorers, Manhattan was a hilly, forested island populated by a Native American tribe called the Manates. (Manhattan Island's name comes from the Indian name *Man-a-hat-ta*, which means land of hills.) The Italian explorer Giovanni da Verrazano was the first European to enter New York harbor in 1524, although he never set foot on land, but traded with the natives who came out to investigate. He brought back reports to his patron, the King of France of the wonderful natural harbor, friendly natives, and rich agricultural lands to the west.

In 1609, Henry Hudson, under the employ of the Dutch East India Company and looking for a passage to the east, explored the entire coastal area and most of the way up the river that now bears his name. Shortly thereafter, other explorers and traders followed, and soon a thriving trade in furs began between the Dutch and the Indians. In 1621 the Dutch West India Company was formed primarily by fur traders to exploit this trade. In 1623, the first Dutch settlers arrived and settled on Governor's Island. As more arrived, the Dutch West India Company established a settlement on the southern tip of Manhattan at the current site of Battery Park. Peter Minuit was appointed as the colony's director and according to legend bought Manhattan Island from the indigenous residents for 24 dollars worth of trinkets; Minuit paid slightly more—about 60 guilders or $40.

The Dutch promptly renamed it New Amsterdam. In 1653 Peter Stuyvesant, the new director, built a fence along present-day Wall Street to protect New Amsterdam from British incursion during a war between England and the Netherlands. Ultimately, King Charles II of England decided to seize New Netherland (New York colony). In 1664 his brother, James the Duke of York entered New Amsterdam harbor with four gunboats and demanded the surrender of the village. Stuyvesant's efforts to rally the citizens of New Amsterdam failed because the community decided that it was better to surrender and be allowed to keep their wealth than to fight and lose everything. The British took over without firing a shot and the Duke of York renamed New Netherland and New Amsterdam with the same name—New York.

Nine years later Britain and the Netherlands went to war again. This time the Dutch were the invading force. They sailed their warships into the harbor and retook New York City. The city was again renamed—this time New Orange, after the Dutch prince William of Orange. However, when the war ended a year later, New Orange was returned to England as part of the peace treaty. The name was changed back to New York and so it remained.

The colony of New York and the other Eastern colonies grew fairly peacefully under the jurisdiction of the British crown until the British decided, in 1765, it was time to tax the colonies to defray the costs of defending the English territories in the New World against French aggression. In spite of the fact that the taxes were negligible compared to what London citizens were paying at the time, the colonists considered them very unfair because unlike the citizens of London, the colonists had no representatives in Parliament and therefore no say in how they were governed.

It wasn't long before the colonists banded together to resist the taxes and started taking out their displeasure on the tax collectors. That caused King George to send troops to protect his tax collectors and English property. Further resistance by the colonists to the English attempt to regain control of their colonies ultimately led to the Declaration of Independence and American Revolution in 1776.

Because of its strategic importance, control of New York City was a key objective for both sides. Unfortunately, early in the war the colonists were unable to hold the city in the face of the overwhelming superiority of British forces, and the British occupied the city during the entire war. In 1781 the British surrendered at Yorktown and the British army finally withdrew from New York City in 1783 after seven years of occupation.

After the Revolutionary War, New York City became the first capital city of the United States. In 1789 the old city hall was renamed Federal Hall and became the nation's first capitol building. George Washington, standing on an open-air balcony, took the oath of office to become the nation's first president.

The opening of the Erie Canal in 1825 caused explosive growth in New York City and the surrounding areas. Modern New York City was formed in 1898 with the unification of Manhattan and the other five boroughs, an event that increased the city's area tenfold and doubled the population to make it the world's second largest city, after London.

New York City has continued to prosper, and today it is the most populous city in America as well as the economic center of the world. This vibrant city has had some tough times along the way, but throughout its history it has been well served by an excellent location, visionary leaders, and hard-working citizens.

Privately owned in the 18th century and known as Bedloe's Island, Liberty Island was acquired by the State of New York and is governed under the jurisdiction of New York City. It is located off the tip of Manhattan and transportation is via the Circle Line from Battery Park in Manhattan or Liberty State Park in New Jersey. Open every day of the year except Christmas, there is no fee for visitors to Liberty or Ellis Island save the cost of the ferry ride.

The Statue of Liberty was a gift from France to the United States. Construction of the statue was begun in Paris, France, in 1875. Frederic Bartholdi designed and supervised the construction of the exterior. Gustave Eiffel engineered the statue's skeleton to support the 100-ton weight of her copper shell and to withstand the high winds of New York Bay. Ten years later it was shipped to the United States in 350 pieces in 214 crates. After a year to assemble, "Liberty Enlightening the World" was unveiled on October 28, 1886. Clad in a beautifully oxidized copper skin, the statue towers 151 feet one inch from base to torch (305 feet one inch from pedestal to torch) and weighs 225 tons. Her garment consists of about 4,000 square yards of "cloth," her index finger is eight feet long, and her mouth is three feet wide. The crown, reached by ascending 354 steps or 22 stories, has 25 windows and is topped with seven rays, said to represent the seven seas and continents of the world. Liberty crushes the chains of slavery under her feet and the tablet in her left hand is inscribed with the date of the Declaration of Independence, July 4, 1776 (in Roman numerals). Emma Lazarus' famous poem, "The New Colossus," is engraved on a tablet on the statue's pedestal.

In 1892 the United States Bureau of Immigration opened Ellis Island to receive and screen immigrants to America. Of the 17 million immigrants that arrived at the Port of New York, approximately 12 million were admitted through Ellis Island, the majority between 1892 and 1924. In 1907, the peak year, 1,285,349 people were admitted. Immigrants came to escape religious or political persecution, war, and famine, to join family members who came before them, or to make their fortune in the New World. After 1924, immigration quotas stemmed the tide and precluded the need for a mass processing center. From 1917 to 1919 and again from 1941 to 1954 Ellis Island served as a detention and deportation center for undesirable aliens. It was closed as an immigration station in 1954. In 1965 President Johnson recognized Liberty and Ellis islands as joint landmarks and made them part of Statue of Liberty National Monument. In 1976 Ellis Island was opened to the public on a limited basis until it was closed in 1984 for a privately financed $160 million restoration, completed in 1990.

Immigrants arrived at Ellis Island indirectly. The steamships that carried them across the Atlantic docked first at piers in New Jersey or Manhattan. First- and second-class passengers were processed on board ship. Steerage, or third-class, passengers were loaded onto other vessels for the journey to Ellis Island. After checking their belongings, they were herded upstairs into the 171-foot-long Great Hall with its barrel-vaulted ceiling. As they progressed toward their physical inspection, doctors used blue chalk to mark some as suspects for closer examination: "E" for eyes, "L" for limp, "X" for insanity. The station shown (four cupola-topped towers) was built in 1900 after fire destroyed the original timber buildings. This massive brick and limestone hall that once housed offices, exam rooms, and dormitories is now a museum. The American Family Immigration History Center in the museum provides information on more than 17 million people who immigrated through the Port of New York from 1892 to 1924 and is accessible via the Internet.

Governor's Island, so named because it was the site of residences for both Dutch and British governors, is located one-half mile from the tip of Manhattan and was used as a military facility for over 200 years. Until recently, it was home of the nation's largest Coast Guard facility. A redevelopment plan that preserves the island's historic and scenic resources is in progress.

A panoramic view of Battery Park on the southern tip of Manhattan and New York Harbor. The most prominent buildings in the skyline are Manhattan's tallest, the World Trade Center towers. The financial district, now dominated by skyscrapers, was once the site of the original Dutch settlement and later the primary residential enclave of post-Revolutionary New York.

Castle Clinton was built as a fort prior to the War of 1812. It had eight-foot thick walls and twenty-eight 32-pounders set into embrasures, but was never used in a battle and was decommissioned in 1823. It became a concert venue called Castle Garden, where, in the musical event of the century, Jenny Lind made her American debut introduced by P.T. Barnum. The sold-out concert also introduced "ticket scalping." From 1855 it served as an immigrant-processing depot until Ellis Island took over this role in 1892. The fort stood on a small island connected to Manhattan by a short causeway until the water around the causeway was filled in to create Battery Park in 1870. Castle Clinton was remodeled in 1896 and served as the New York City Aquarium until that moved to Coney Island in 1941. Ultimately it was declared a national historic monument and now serves as a tourist information center.

Bowling Green was originally a parade ground and marketplace. Broadway originates at Bowling Green and extends 150 miles—the entire length of Manhattan and all the way to Albany, making it one of the longest streets in the world. The short building lower-right is Cass Gilbert's U.S. Custom House at Broadway and Bowling Green, now the Smithsonian's National Museum of the American Indian. In the center is 26 Broadway, former headquarters of John D. Rockefeller's Standard Oil Trust from 1885 until the 1900s. When the trust was dissolved, it became the headquarters of Standard Oil of New Jersey (now Exxon) until the 1930s, when it moved to Rockefeller Center. It is a fine example of a classical skyscraper with dramatic three-story high Ionic columns on the base and above on the tower. It is topped by an immense bronze tripod shaped like an oil lamp, which conceals a chimney, and is notable for having the first push-button elevator. Chase Manhattan and the 71-story 40 Wall Street tower over it.

Wall Street's name derives from a wooden palisade fence built by the Dutch on the town's northern border to guard against British encroachment. In 1699, when the wall was removed, the name was given to the parallel road. The southern half of the district is the site of the original Dutch settlement and the oldest neighborhood in the city. It is home to the world's largest concentration of banks, brokerage firms, and financial institutions, as well as the New York Stock Exchange and the American Stock Exchange. The building in the center is the Bank of New York, originally Irving Trust Company, at 1 Wall Street, named in honor of Washington Irving and built on the site of one of his former domiciles. The building's series of setbacks adds to its verticality and makes this 1931 bank tower appear taller than its 50-story height. Nevertheless, it is dwarfed by the City Bank-Farmers Trust tower, directly behind it. On their left is the squat ziggurat-topped 15 Broad Street, also known as Equitable Trust Company, built in 1928.

Wall Street has been a financial center for over 200 years and most of the buildings were home to banks or insurance companies. From top right, the black glass building in the corner is the Marine Midland Bank next to the Equitable Building. Directly in front are the Realty and Trinity buildings, built in the Gothic style to complement neighboring Trinity Church. The Trinity and Realty buildings have a connecting wrought-iron footbridge joining them at their upper stories. Built at a cost of $15 million, they were the costliest commercial structures of their era. The seven-story gold-ribbed pyramid-topped building (center, top) is Banker's Trust, also known as 16 Wall Street, formed by New York City financiers as their safeguard against monopolistic trusts. It was the second largest trust in the country and controlled almost three-quarters of all credit and capital in the United States.

The Equitable Building, at 120 Broadway between Pine and Cedar, is one of the skyscrapers responsible for the cliché "concrete canyons." When erected in 1915, the city did not have any zoning ordinances and the developers constructed this 42-story tower straight up from the building line without any setbacks, effectively blocking out sunlight from the streets below and casting a seven-acre shadow. It accommodated 16,000 workers and was the world's largest office building upon completion. A year after its construction, the city wrote the country's first zoning law, which required setbacks for skyscrapers and regulated the relationship between a building's height and the area that it could occupy. The building's unusual H-shape and two-story penthouse are highlighted in this aerial perspective.

A late afternoon view shows Trinity Church (Broadway and Wall) casting its shadow on the neighboring office building. Trinity Church was the city's tallest building for nearly 50 years at 280 feet, and its spire dominated the skyline. Now neighboring office buildings dwarf it. Although one of New York City's oldest buildings, this is actually the third Trinity Church. The first, built in 1698, was destroyed in the Great Fire of 1776, which consumed much of the city. The second was torn down because of structural problems. This structure was completed in 1846 by the founder of the American Institute of Architects, Richard Upjohn, and is a classic example of Gothic Revival architecture. In the adjacent cemetery one can find the tomb of Alexander Hamilton, the first memorial to unknown servicemen of the Revolutionary War, and gravestones for Albert Gallatin and William Bradford.

This view from the TriBeCa (the Triangle Below Canal) looks past City Hall Park and the Woolworth Building all the way to the East River. TriBeCa, once an industrial and warehouse district, is now a community of art galleries and restaurants.

South Street Seaport is a 12-square block landmark historic district that recalls a time when lower Manhattan's East River was a thriving seaport. The district combines the historic and commercial with cobblestone streets, 19th century buildings, and the Fulton Fish Market (the city's busiest fishmonger). Pier 17 is a shopping arcade with restaurants; the building directly behind it across FDR Drive is the South Street Seaport Museum. The ships moored at Piers 15 and 16 (not all shown, as some still sail) exemplify an era when this part of town was the center of shipping and commerce for New York and the rest of world. They include the four-masted bark *Peking* (1911); the *Ambrose* lightship (1908); an iron full-rigged British trade ship the *Wavertree* (1855); the cargo schooner *Pioneer* (1885); the wooden fishing schooner the *Lettie G. Howard* (1893); and the ferryboat *W.O. Decker* (1930). At the end of the pier is a sightseeing Circle Line boat. In the late 1800s shipping moved to the deeper harbors of the Hudson to accommodate larger vessels.

BATTERY PARK CITY

Battery Park City is bounded by West Street and the Hudson River and Pier A and Chambers Street. The land on which this development was built was reclaimed from New York Bay and transformed into modern apartment complexes, restaurants, shops, office towers, hotels, entertainment venues, coves, and a yacht harbor. It was intentionally designed with low-rise buildings, parks, and a waterfront promenade to offset the density of the neighboring commercial office towers. The round building in the foreground is the Museum of Jewish Heritage, a memorial to and history of the Holocaust.

Cesar Pelli designed this complex of four commercial towers, two gatehouses, and public space in the middle of Battery Park City. This view looks north from the South Cove, with the Museum of Jewish Heritage in the foreground. The complex is actually adjacent to the North Cove Yacht Harbor (not shown) and extends from Vesey Street to Albany Street.

New York City's skyline along the Hudson River is dominated by the city's tallest structure, the 110-story World Trade Center towers. The observation decks on the 107th (indoor) and 110th (outdoor) floors are a favorite tourist attraction, where on a clear day you can see more than 55 miles from a height of over 1,300 feet. In the foreground are the residential towers of Battery Park City interspersed with commercial developments such as the four World Financial Center towers.

This trio of modern office towers shows how they overshadow the district's early buildings and skyscrapers. The building to the left is Battery Park Plaza, in the middle is 17 State Street, and to the right is 1 State Street Plaza. Early beauties such as the Cass Gilbert's U.S. Custom House and the green top of 40 Wall Street peek out around the edges. The Battery was originally an open area reserved for a battery of cannons, which gave Battery Park its name.

ST. PAUL'S CHAPEL

Built in 1766 on Broadway, between Fulton and Vesey streets, St. Paul's Chapel is the city's oldest church and the only intact pre-Revolutionary War building that remains in constant use. The Broadway entrance was a rear entrance, with the main entrance located under the tower. The gilded interior is lit by 14 Waterford chandeliers. George Washington worshipped here and after his inauguration as first president of the United States, he was officially received at St. Paul's.

The construction of the headquarters of the F.W. Woolworth Company in 1913 was a major national event. From the White House, Woodrow Wilson threw the switch that illuminated over 5,000 windows. Located at 233 Broadway, between Barclay Street and Park Place, it was the tallest building in the world for 16 years until the Chrysler building surpassed it in 1930, itself surpassed by the Empire State Building in 1931. The ornate marble lobby, designed like a church nave—along with the fact that Woolworth paid the $13 million cost in cash—helped give rise to its nickname, "The Cathedral of Commerce." Architect Cass Gilbert abandoned the popular Beaux-Arts style for the flamboyant Gothic Revival style. The granite base is topped by two stories of limestone and the rest is terra cotta, which allowed for its elaborate lacy ornamentation. This 60-story, 792-foot-high beauty is adorned with allegorical figures, gargoyles, and mythical beasts. The ornate interior includes a vaulted three-story-high glass mosaic ceiling, and gargoyles that caricature people associated with the building's construction, including one of Woolworth himself, bent over and counting his nickels and dimes.

A number of state and city agencies are located in the downtown's northern section. In the center, at City Hall Park between Park Row and Broadway, is City Hall, the seat of New York City government since 1812. It is an excellent example of early 19th century architecture with its central portico topped by a cupola clock tower and a 6,000-pound bell. When originally built, the governor used inferior brownstone instead of marble on the building's rear side in order to save money with the rationale that so few people lived uptown it would hardly be noticed. In the fifties both were stripped off and replaced with limestone and granite front and back. Once situated in an open area used as the town commons, skyscrapers now ring it. Behind it is the New York City Courthouse, also known as Tweed Courthouse because Boss Tweed, head of the most notorious political machine in New York City history, and his cronies pocketed millions in kickbacks during its construction.

The Municipal Building, on the right in this photo, with its flattened U-shape, has all the elements of a classic skyscraper: an elaborate base of Corinthian columns topped by a plain shaft and a capital that is a series of temples shaped into a tower. The small photo provides a closer look at the ten-story colonnaded tower on the building's top, ornamented with such neoclassical elements as balustrades, urns, obelisks, pyramidal domes, and a miniature choragic monument capped by a 25-foot-high gilded statue of "Civic Fame" with the city's coat of arms in her right arm and the city's crown in her left. The building was created at 1 Centre Street in 1914 to accommodate the need for expanded city government offices following the incorporation of the boroughs into New York City. Because of its immense size, people often mistake this for City Hall. To its left is the gold pyramid-topped U.S. Courthouse by Cass Gilbert and the New York State Supreme Court on the far left. In the foreground is the Javits Federal Office Building at Foley Square. The approach to Brooklyn Bridge and South Street Seaport are visible in the background.

The dramatic hexagonal building with its enormous Corinthian portico is the New York State Supreme Court, circa 1913. The building's shape was the winning design to address an irregularly shaped plot. Above it, with its trademark gold pyramid top obscured, is the Cass Gilbert-designed 1936 United States Courthouse. The completion of the courthouses put an end to the infamous crime-ridden slum district known as Five Points—named for the intersection of three streets. Five Points was the scene of daily murders and the stomping ground of notorious gangs such as the "Plug Uglies," who wore stuffed or plug hats as helmets when going into battle. The most recent addition to the area is the Federal Office Building, top right.

Overlooking City Hall Park, when completed in 1899 the 386-foot, 31-story Park Row Building was the world's highest and New York's second skyscraper. Located at 15 Park Row, between Ann and Beekman streets, it includes many ornamental details such as numerous balustraded balconies, a three-story colonnade topped by two circular copper-covered cupola temples adorned with figures. Slightly visible are four colossal caryatids near the building's base.

With lower Manhattan and the Municipal Building visible in the foreground, this aerial view shows the approach to the Brooklyn Bridge from Park Row in Manhattan over the East River to Cadman Place, Brooklyn, on the opposite shore. Brooklyn's history begins with the waterfront hamlet of Fulton Ferry, which Robert Fulton's steam ferry, in 1814, made a gateway to Brooklyn and Long Island as well. The yellow two-story shingled fireboat station in the shadow of the Brooklyn Bridge and adjacent to the upscale River Café is the Fulton Ferry Museum, which traces the history of the harbor and seafaring. Ferryboats serviced the Hudson since 1600s and lasted until 1924, but ferry service began its decline after the building of the Brooklyn Bridge in 1883.

The Brooklyn Bridge was a marvel of engineering and was declared the eighth wonder of the world upon its completion. Its 1883 opening was a major event and was attended by such crowds that 12 people died in a stampede when someone falsely sounded an alarm that the bridge was collapsing. It was designed by John Roebling, the inventor of wire cable, who suffered a fatal accident in the early stages of the bridge's construction, and completed by his son, Augustus, who became an invalid from a disabling attack of the bends caused by working underwater to supervise the excavation of the bridge's footings. He supervised the final construction stages from his wheelchair—crippled, half-paralyzed, and partially blind—from a Brooklyn apartment armed with a pair of binoculars. The close-up shows the dramatic Gothic granite towers and cables, each composed of 5,296 galvanized steel wires. The bridge's roadbed is composed entirely of steel, an engineering first for a bridge of its size.

MANHATTAN AND BROOKLYN BRIDGES

Two bridges connect lower Manhattan to Brooklyn. The Brooklyn Bridge was built in 1883 and the Manhattan Bridge (foreground) was built in 1909. Brooklyn Heights Promenade and the Navy Yard are visible on the Brooklyn side and South Street Seaport and Lower East side high-rises can be seen on the Manhattan side. DUMBO, an acronym for Down Under Manhattan Bridge Overpass, is the site of many lofts. There is a pedestrian walkway across the Brooklyn Bridge.

VIEW FROM WALL STREET LOOKING UPTOWN
This view from the financial district shows the demarcation between the
skyscrapers of Downtown and Midtown separated by the primarily residential
areas of the Village, Chelsea, and the Lower East Side.

The old Police Headquarters Building—240 Centre Street at Broome and Grand streets—on the Lower East Side was built for and served as police headquarters from 1905 to 1973, when the police department relocated to 1 Police Plaza. The city could not find a suitable use for the building and sold it in 1987. It was converted into luxury cooperative apartments.

The grand entrance to the bridge is located at Canal Street and Bowery. The arch, framed by colonnades on either side, is one of three triumphal arches in the city. (The others are Washington Square Arch and the Soldiers' and Sailors' Monument in Brooklyn.) To the left of the arch is Sara Delano Roosevelt Park. Along with Tompkins Square Park, it is one of largest parks on the Lower East Side and includes playgrounds, two wading pools, a roller skating rink, basketball courts, a senior citizens' center, bird garden, and vendors' market bounded by a perimeter of shade trees and benches. To the right of the arch is a public housing development, Confucius Plaza, in Chinatown. Located on the Lower East Side of Manhattan is the largest Chinatown in the United States with the greatest concentration of Chinese in the western hemisphere in the two square miles bounded by Kenmore and Delancey on the north and East and Worth streets on the south.

MANHATTAN BRIDGE

Looking north from Brooklyn, Manhattan Bridge crosses the East River from Tillary Street at Flatbush Avenue in Brooklyn to Canal Street at Bowery, Manhattan. It is one of the main links to Brooklyn. The subway's B and D trains go to Brooklyn via the Manhattan Bridge and provide a great perspective of the East River and the Manhattan skyline.

The park occupies land that was originally the site of the city gallows and a potter's field until the cemetery closed in 1823 and the public square opened. Inset is Greenwich Village's most famous landmark: Washington Square Arch, the literal gateway to Fifth Avenue. The arch was first constructed of wood in 1889 to celebrate the centennial of George Washington's inauguration. When the decision to make a permanent arch was made, Stanford White got the commission. It is 86 feet high with a span of 30 feet two inches.

New York University was founded in 1831 with the intent of providing a practical education to people aspiring to professional careers. The university's first president was Albert Gallatin, Thomas Jefferson's secretary of treasury. The university includes 13 colleges at five locations in Manhattan, along with branch campuses. The campus buildings are framed by SoHo in the foreground and Washington Square Arch in the top left corner. To its right are the library and the Stern School of Business, with Washington Square Village's graduate student housing in front. The beige towers house faculty. To their right is the NYU rec center with tennis courts on top and a pool and fitness center below.

Greenwich Village, bounded by Broadway, Houston, and 14th streets, has been home to students, artists, and the avant-garde since the mid-nineteenth century. Tiny green parks, brick townhomes, and low-rise buildings characterize it, partly because its softer soil did not lend itself to skyscrapers like the more solid granite found at the southern tip and center of the island. The English christened the neighborhood Greenwich in 1712 after the English salt-making village of the same name.

Originally part of a larger parkland named Union Place, Union Square Park was redesigned as a smaller park and renamed in 1832. The fountain in the center commemorates completion of the city's waterworks, which improved public health. In the foreground is an equestrian statue of George Washington marking the site where the general met with New York City's citizens after the 1783 evacuation of the city by the British. The Village lies below 14th Street. The streets above 14th and Canal streets were developed along a grid plan. Above 14th is the Chelsea District on the West Side and Gramercy Park and Union Square Park districts on the East Side.

Zeckendorf Plaza is bounded by Irving Place and Union Square and E. 14th and 15th streets. The four Zeckendorf Towers sit in front of the Con Ed building. Consolidated Edison built this 23-story office tower in 1926 as a memorial to the company's employees who died in World War I. Atop the building is a colonnaded temple with an eight-foot–high lantern. Behind it is Union Square Park.

Built on the former site of an 1806 arsenal, Madison Square Park was officially opened in 1847. The demolished arsenal was replaced by another arsenal at 64th and Fifth—one of two Central Park structures that predate the park. The seven-acre statue-filled park provides great views of three of the city's oldest skyscrapers on different square corners—the New York Life Insurance Building, the Met Life Insurance Tower, and the Flatiron. In the foreground is the Flatiron Building where Broadway cuts across Fifth Avenue at 23rd Street. In 1845 a volunteer fireman created the official rules of baseball and reputedly the city's first baseball games were played in the vicinity of the park.

The 1902 Flatiron Building located at the junction of Broadway and Fifth Avenue, with its spine facing 23rd Street, is considered the city's first steel-framed structure and skyscraper and is its oldest remaining skyscraper. Originally called the Fuller Building, it was nicknamed the Flatiron because of its distinctive wedge shape. Located at the end of one of the city's most fashionable shopping districts—"Ladies' Mile" along Broadway and Sixth Avenue—the corner of 23rd was infamous for its gusty winds, exacerbated by the building's downdrafts. Vintage postcards show men standing on the corner watching women's skirts blow over their heads. A policeman was stationed there to disperse crowds of loitering men. Legend has it that the policeman would admonish oglers with the warning, "Hey you on Twenty-three, skidoo."

NEW YORK LIFE INSURANCE BUILDING

The New York Life Insurance Company Building with its golden pyramid-shaped tower resides on the spot of the original Madison Square Gardens. Cass Gilbert designed the 33-story building in 1928. To its right are the Metropolitan Life Insurance Building and Metropolitan Life Insurance Tower.

The beautiful 1909 Met Life Tower building is partially obscured by scaffolding as it undergoes renovation. The 350-foot tower is an enlarged bell tower modeled after St. Mark's campanile in Venice. An elaborate lantern sits atop a high sloping roof. The building is distinctively dotted with windows from base to tower, and all four sides of the tower are graced with an enormous clockface: 26.5 feet in diameter with a 17-foot-long minute hand. On the tower's left sits the 11-story Metropolitan Life Insurance North Building; the squat structure was intended as the base of a mammoth skyscraper until the stock market crash derailed plans.

The distinctive gold tower of the New York Life Insurance Company building exemplifies the expense and extra ornamentation characteristic of the city's older skyscrapers. The roof's eight-sided pinnacle was originally covered with gold leaf, but pollutants caused deterioration, and in 1967 it was replaced with a new roof finished with brilliant gold-colored ceramic tiles. Long a fixture of New York's skyline, the building celebrated its 70th anniversary in 1998. Since 1985 it has been lit at night. Architect Cass Gilbert nicknamed the building the Cathedral of Insurance. The building is the home office of New York Life Insurance Company, a Fortune 100 company, and one of the largest insurance and financial service companies in the world.

MIDTOWN

The Empire State Building, Fifth Avenue and E. 34th, dominates this view of Midtown Manhattan. The 102-story Art Deco masterpiece was built during the Great Depression and completed in a mere 12 months and 45 days—the fastest-rising skyscraper ever at the rate of four and a half stories per week. The Empire State Building was the result of a competition between two auto moguls—John Jakob Raskob of General Motors and Walter Chrysler of the Chrysler Corporation—to build the tallest building. Capped off in 1931 at 1,250 feet, it was the nation's tallest building until 1972 when it lost this status to the World Trade Center Towers, which in turn lost it to the Sears Tower in Chicago. Fittingly for such a record-breaking building, the concourse level includes a Guinness World Records Exhibit Hall with such arcana as the world's most expensive shoes, the biggest Raggedy Ann doll, and a life-sized statue of Robert Wadlow, at eight feet 11 inches, the world's tallest man.

This close-up of King Kong's favorite perch highlights the 204-foot antenna that was originally conceived of as a dirigible mooring mast and that propelled the finished height of the building beyond that of the Chrysler Building. Built at a cost of over $40 million, including the land, the building includes 6,500 windows, 73 elevators, and 2.5 million feet of electrical wire. Every month 100 tons of trash is removed from the building. Fitness buffs can tackle the annual Empire State Building Run-up—102 floors and 1,860 steps from street level to the 102nd floor. This view also shows the innovative use of metal to frame the windows, which adds to the building's verticality. In the 1970s, the top 30 stories were illuminated. Colored lights are used on seasonal days—red and white for Valentine's Day, green for St. Patrick's Day, and red, white, and blue for the Fourth of July.

Located on the Hudson River and bounded by W. 17th and W. 23rd Streets and West Street, Chelsea Piers is a year-round sports complex with six separate facilities that include a sports center, golf club, and indoor driving range, roller rinks, sky rink, field house, and bowling lanes.

Directly behind the train yards is Madison Square Garden, which occupies the site of the former Penn Station. Behind is the hulking black Met Life building with the Empire State Building behind again and to its left. Now trains arrive and depart from a space under the Garden.

Madison Square Garden is located at the northwest corner of Midtown South at Seventh Avenue between W. 31st and W. 33rd. This round indoor sports arena is home to the New York Knicks NBA basketball team. Behind it, the 57-story black glass slab tower of 1 Penn Plaza dominates the neighborhood. The main post office building on the far left faces Eighth Avenue.

Located at 295 Madison Avenue, this 45-story, 537-foot tall Art Deco skyscraper was built in 1929. Abraham Lefcourt, a developer, hired Charles F. Mayer to design it.

Opened in 1902, Macy's grew through a series of additions in the 1920s and 30s to encompass an entire city block, Sixth Avenue and Broadway and W. 34th and W. 35th Streets. It is the world's largest department store with over two million feet of floor space. Since the 1920s it has sponsored the Macy's Thanksgiving Day Parade, a New York and American tradition.

The dark-glass convention center was designed by I.M. Pei and is visible in the rear center of the photo at the water's edge. The five-block long building stretches from West 34th to 39th streets and is conveniently located near the Lincoln Tunnel and the Port Authority Bus Terminal. It includes a 60,000 square foot gallery, exhibition hall, and pavilion overlooking the Hudson River. To the left are the train yards leading into Madison Square Garden and in the foreground is the Garment District.

The Port Authority Bus Terminal between Eighth and Ninth avenues and W. 40th and W. 42nd streets opened in 1950 and is the nation's busiest bus terminal. It operates three dozen bus lines, which serve over 57 million passengers annually. In a typical week the terminal handles some 7,200 buses carrying almost 190,000 passengers. Above the terminal's roof is a three-story superstructure that accommodates parking for over 1,000 cars. To the left of the terminal is the old McGraw-Hill Building, now the Health Insurance Building. The distinctive green-blue terra cotta-clad McGraw-Hill Building was designed by Raymond Hood who, along with his partner, also won the competition to build the Chicago Tribune Tower.

The infamous Hell's Kitchen, roughly bounded by the Hudson River and Eighth Avenue and West 30th to 57th streets, is home to such uninviting landmarks as the Lincoln Tunnel Entrance and the Port Authority Bus Terminal. Though developers have tried to erase the 1930s and 40s Irish working class stigma of the neighborhood by gentrifying its name to Clinton, the old name of Hell's Kitchen persists. The north-south roadway through the photo's center is Ninth Avenue. At top right is the 1989 pyramid-topped, two-toned Worldwide Plaza, which occupies an entire city block and was conceived of as a way to demarcate the dense commercial sector from the primarily residential neighborhoods nearby. The roadway cutting across the center of the picture is the approach to the Port Authority Bus Terminal. The area in between comprises the city's Theater District.

U.S.S. *Intrepid* in harbor with the West Side waterfront and neighborhood and three modern-day skyscrapers—CitySpire, 1 Worldwide Plaza, and 1585 Broadway—in the background. The aircraft carrier U.S.S. *Intrepid*, with vintage and modern aircraft parked on the flight deck, is the centerpiece of a flotilla of exhibits at the Intrepid Sea-Air Museum, located at Pier 86, W. 46th and 12th Avenue. Construction of the *Intrepid* began six days before the attack on Pearl Harbor and the ship saw 37 years of illustrious service. The *Intrepid* and her air wing fought many World War II campaigns in the Pacific Ocean and sank 200 enemy ships and destroyed over 600 planes. The ship was also the primary recovery vessel for two manned space flights in the 1960s and served during the Korean and Vietnam conflicts. Docked nearby are the missile submarine U.S.S. *Growler* (inset top) and a destroyer, the U.S.S. *Edison*.

Times Square in midtown Manhattan is located at the intersection of 42nd Street, Broadway, and Seventh Avenue. Crowded day and night since the 1900s it has been home to the city's major theater district with over 30 major theaters located nearby. Tourists might find it helpful to note that a Visitor's Center is located at 1560 Broadway.

Times Square takes its name from the Times Tower building formerly occupied by *The New York Times*. This neon heart of Manhattan has been experiencing a major renovation, some say a "Disneyfication," to make the area cleaner, safer, and more attractive.

PARAMOUNT BUILDING

This pre-Colombian-style 1927 building located in the heart of Times Square was headquarters for the Famous Players-Lasky Corporation, forerunner of entertainment giant Paramount Pictures. The glass globe on top—emblematic of Paramount's worldwide reach—and the clocks' faces are illuminated at night. The clocks incorporate Paramount's trademark five-pointed star instead of numerals.

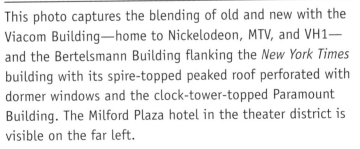

This photo captures the blending of old and new with the Viacom Building—home to Nickelodeon, MTV, and VH1—and the Bertelsmann Building flanking the *New York Times* building with its spire-topped peaked roof perforated with dormer windows and the clock-tower-topped Paramount Building. The Milford Plaza hotel in the theater district is visible on the far left.

Helmut Jahn's CitySpire at 150 W. 56th Street has earned its place as a recognizable addition to the cityscape. After a series of setbacks it culminates in a dome-topped octagonal tower. The mixed use 69-story building houses offices on the lower levels and luxury apartments on the top. To the left of CitySpire is Carnegie Tower, which was added to Carnegie Hall in 1986. The six-story Carnegie Hall was financed by steel magnate Andrew Carnegie and opened in May 1891 with a concert by Peter Ilyich Tchaikovsky and Walter Damrosch. It is renowned for its outstanding acoustics and the diverse talent it has attracted to perform there, such as John Philip Sousa, Gustav Mahler, Booker T. Washington, Ignace Jan Paderewski, the Beatles, Judy Garland, Paul Robeson, Leonard Bernstein, Ella Fitzgerald, Yo-Yo Ma, Jessye Norman, and Mark Twain. When threatened with demolition in the 1960s, the late violinist Isaac Stern led a drive to save the building and after a major renovation it was placed on the National Register of Historic Places.

On the left is the postmodern pink three-tiered Equitable Center Tower West. The archway on the apex of its tower are the boardroom's windows. An enormous work by Roy Lichtenstein in the building's five-story atrium is worth a trip inside. The building is connected to Rockefeller Center's underground concourse. In the photo's center is the 42-story horizontal-striped 1585 Broadway with its glass roof shaped like a cut pyramid.

MIDTOWN AND THE EAST RIVER
The East 50s is the center of the Midtown Manhattan business district. The Empire State Building at Fifth Avenue and E. 34th marks Midtown on the southern edge.

This aerial view provides perspective on the juxtaposition of the New York Public Library (center left), Bryant Park, and the surrounding neighborhood. Bryant Park, behind the New York Public Library, includes a restaurant and food stands. The Croton Reservoir was drained to create a site for the New York Public Library. Opened in 1847 as Reservoir Park, Bryant Park was renamed in honor of William Cullen Bryant, who used his position as editor of the *New York Evening Post* to promote the creation of Central Park. The library is famous for "Patience" and "Fortitude," two recumbent lions flanking the stairs, so-named by Fiorello LaGuardia in the 1930s to represent the qualities New Yorkers would need to survive the economic depression. On the library's left side is the American Standard Building, also known as the American Radiator Building, and above it is 500 Fifth Avenue, an office tower.

The library's collection of 52 million books, manuscripts, maps, photographs, periodicals, newspapers, microfilms, prints, paintings, ephemera, CD-ROMs, videos, and online resources make it one of the world's great reference libraries. Among its treasures are a Gutenberg Bible, Shakespeare's first five folios, ancient Torah scrolls, Jefferson's handwritten copy of the Declaration of Independence, a handwritten copy of George Washington's Farewell Inaugural Address to his troops, and Alexander Hamilton's handwritten draft of the U.S. Constitution. Founded in 1895 with the private libraries of James Lenox and John Jacob Astor and monies from the Samuel Tilden foundation, it was opened to the public by President Taft in 1911.

The American Radiator Building has a striking color scheme designed to symbolize the transformation of coal into energy, which was the American Radiator company's business. The first story is dark bronze and polished black granite; above the black brick is gold terra-cotta trim and a golden crown. Designed in 1923 by Raymond Hood, this was his first major New York commission and helped to establish his reputation as a leading architect in the United States.

The Metropolitan Life Building (also known as Pan Am) and the Chrysler Building dominate this view from Midtown East looking toward Central Park and the West and East sides. Between the two skyscrapers is the blunt buttressed crown of the 56-story Art Deco Chanin Building. Grand Central is almost obscured by 101 Park Avenue in the foreground.

Continuing the view from the facing page, the slanted Citibank roofline takes its place along with the Chrysler Building as one of the instantly identifiable landmarks in this part of town. Just visible to the far right of Citibank is the Queensboro Bridge and Roosevelt Island, which marks the start of the Upper East Side.

This 77-story elaborate Art Deco masterpiece, with its unmistakable stainless steel skin is one of New York City's most beloved and recognizable landmarks. Its 197-foot seven-tier spire was constructed in secret and hoisted in place thorough the roof opening. Once installed, the Chrysler Building surpassed the Eiffel Tower to become the world's tallest building in 1930 measuring 1,046 feet high. Unfortunately, the Empire State Building surpassed it in height a mere two months later. The building is loaded with whimsical touches such as cars on the building's corners, a stainless steel pinnacle based on a Chrysler radiator cap, and gargoyles based on Chrysler hood ornaments. The inset shows the tower with pairs of eagles—automobile-derived ornamental details—on all four corners and the stainless steel arcs with triangular windows that are brilliantly illuminated at night.

Although the black Met Life building built in 1963 hulks over it, the Helmsley and its highly decorated roof (inset) still manage to dominate the view when looking down Park Avenue. Designed in 1929 as offices for the railroads using Grand Central Terminal and called the New York Central Building, it became the Helmsley Building in 1977. Visible at ground level are archways for Park Avenue traffic and access to Grand Central Terminal.

United Nations Plaza is a complex of office buildings, apartments, and hotels situated on the East River at E. 44th between First and Second avenues, across from Queens. The land that it occupies is considered an international zone and is not part of the United States. The UN Secretariat with its glass slab curtain wall is the dominant building. The low-domed building is the General Assembly Building. The United Nations, established at the end of World War II, was completed in 1953 and was built on 18 acres donated by the Rockefellers.

Built on a bluff overlooking the East River, Tudor City is a high-rise residential complex built around two parks and located near the United Nations and the Ford Foundation. The three main buildings are the dark brown terra-cotta trimmed 22-story Prospect, Tudor, and Windsor towers. Tudor City was developed in 1928 by the Fred French Company as a private effort to revitalize an industrial slum area of slaughterhouses, glue factories, and breweries. Designed to face private open spaces and thus avoid the surrounding smelly and unsightly neighbors, the buildings, as a result, have relatively few windows on their east sides. Conceived of as a self-contained city, the complex of 12 buildings, all in the Tudor Gothic style, includes apartments, hotel rooms, restaurants, shops, a post office, and private parks. Tudor City was a precursor of planned urban communities and is a designated historic district.

Bounded by Fifth and Sixth avenues and W. 48th and W. 51st streets, Rockefeller Center is the largest privately owned business and entertainment complex in the world, as well as a triumph of Art Deco architecture. Fine art abounds in buildings' interiors and exteriors—murals from the WPA, mosaics, and sculptures by Rockwell Kent. This vast 11-acre complex includes 21 high-rise office buildings, some 30 restaurants, Radio City Music Hall—the world's largest indoor theater—TV studios, office space, stores, and convention halls. In the center is 30 Rockefeller Plaza.

The largest (70 stories) and first built (1934) of the skyscrapers of Rockefeller Center, the G.E. Building at 30 Rockefeller Plaza is the centerpiece of the complex. Originally the RCA Building, now General Electric's initials emblazon the rooftop. It is the most public of the Center's buildings and home to two of the most popular tourist attractions: NBC Studios and the recently renovated Rainbow Room, a landmark nightspot for dinner, drinks, and dancing. It faces Fifth Avenue and overlooks the plaza with a sunken courtyard, used as an ice skating rink in winter and a restaurant in the summer. It features an immense eight-ton gilded statue of Prometheus as a centerpiece.

The 54-story Citicorp Building, built in 1977, is a recent addition to the Lexington Avenue skyline. Its distinctive trademark slanted roof versus the traditional flat roof broke new ground and is also a solar energy collector. To its right is another new post-modern Midtown building, 599 Lexington Avenue.

St. Patrick's Cathedral, seat of the Roman Catholic Archdiocese of New York, is the largest Roman Catholic Cathedral in the United States and the 11th largest church in the world. Opened in 1879, it is one of Midtown's most famous landmarks. Its ornate Gothic facade and 132-foot spires stand out amidst the angular lines of Fifth Avenue's surrounding skyscrapers. James Renwick, designer of Washington, D.C.'s Smithsonian castle, was the architect. The Cathedral has massive bronze doors decorated with statues of saints and exquisite stained glass windows.

Philip Johnson and John Burgee's 1984 Sony Building (also known as the AT& T Building) at 550 Madison Avenue is considered by many to be New York City's finest postmodern skyscraper. The broken pediment Chippendale bonnet top and pink granite make the Sony Building stand out in a sea of office towers. The lobby inside is three stories high to accommodate the "Golden Boy" statue that once adorned the former AT&T's headquarters building. Just visible behind the building is the pyramid top of Helmut Jahn's Park Avenue Tower. To Sony's left is Edward Larrabee Barnes' IBM Building. The buildings are located in the heart of Midtown's business district.

A crown jewel of Art Deco New York, the Waldorf-Astoria Hotel at 301 Park Avenue occupies an entire block at the corner of Park and 50th Street. The building's 47 stories are somewhat bland except for the two ornamental towers. The towers contain private luxury apartments and have a private entrance separate from the hotel's 2,000 plus rooms. Herbert Hoover, who lived here for 30 years, was one of many famous residents. The somewhat plain exterior conceals a sensational interior. The hotel's immense ballroom, accommodating 6,000 guests, is one of the city's premiere venues for large social events.

MIDTOWN

In this panoramic view, Midtown Manhattan's skyscrapers vie with each other as they reach toward the sky. Rockefeller Center is on the left with the spires of St. Patrick's Cathedral fighting for attention behind the GE Building. The Times Square district is to the right of the Paramount Building, with one of its two clock faces visible front and center. Across the East River lies Queens.

QUEENSBORO BRIDGE

The East River is spanned by the cantilevered Queensboro Bridge, which connects Midtown Manhattan at 60th Street to Crescent Street in Long Island City, Queens, with Queensbridge Park at the water's edge. Built in 1909, it is referred to by locals as the 59th Street Bridge and was immortalized in song by Simon & Garfunkel. High-rise apartment towers fill the northern and eastern sections of the Queensboro Bridge neighborhood.

Beneath the Queensboro Bridge lies the 1.75-mile-long Roosevelt Island, now the site of an upscale housing development. The island is reached via a tram, or by the footbridge seen in front of the Queensboro Bridge. A shuttle bus takes visitors from the tram station to the other end of the island with its lighthouse and a beautiful park. The island was originally known as Blackwell's Island and later Welfare Island when it was home to a workhouse, orphanage, lunatic asylums, and hospitals for the terminally ill.

The Roosevelt Island Tramway runs between Second Avenue and 60th Street on the Upper East Side and Roosevelt Island. The four-minute ride on the Swiss-made aerial tramway provides great East River vistas. Below the tram is the Queensboro Bridge, which includes a footbridge for pedestrian traffic.

The 1921 Crown Building (also known as the Heckscher Building) was the first skyscraper built after the 1916 zoning laws went into effect. Located at the important retail location of Fifth Avenue and 57th, it was the first home of the Museum of Modern Art in 1929. Next door is Tiffany's and adjacent to Tiffany's is Trump Tower. Behind and mostly obscured by the Crown Building is Bergdoff Goodman's.

Built at a cost of $12.5 million in 1907, the Plaza Hotel on Fifth Avenue between 58th and 59th streets was the epitome of luxury when it opened and still retains its cachet. The Goulds and Vanderbilts were some of the first occupants and, like many upper-class clientele, rented suites on long-term leases. The Plaza was also a favorite of Frank Lloyd Wright and le Corbusier, both of whom resided there during stays in the city. Inside the hotel is a huge oil painting of Eloise, in recognition of the fact that the Plaza is the home of this famous children's book heroine. In the foreground is the spire of the Sherry-Netherland Hotel, another grande dame of Fifth Avenue.

CENTRAL PARK PANORAMA

The beautiful green rectangle of Central Park as seen looking north with the Hudson River and the West Side of Manhattan on the left. This view captures the immensity of this famous urban greenbelt designed by Frederick Law Olmsted and Calvert Vaux in 1858 and completed in 1873. It spans 2.5 miles from 59th Street to 110th Street and is a half-mile wide from Seventh Avenue to Eighth Avenue. The first urban landscaped park in the United States, its 843 acres comprise six percent of Manhattan's land area. The 1811 grid plan of Manhattan neglected to designate adequate open space, which by the 1840s threatened to make the city uninhabitable. In 1853 the city began to acquire open space out of the center of the grid plan for the creation of a central park. Before the park's construction could begin, swamps and open sewers had to be drained and pig farms and squatters' shacks had to be cleared out.

BETHESDA FOUNTAIN AND LOEB BOATHOUSE

The Loeb Boathouse and Bethesda Fountain are located at the south
end of the 22.5-acre Lake. The boathouse rents rowboats and
includes a restaurant. The Bethesda Fountain overlooks the Lake and
a 37-acre wooded stretch known as the Ramble—a favorite haunt
for bird watchers. The grandiose fountain with its winged "Angel of
the Waters" is one of the few formal structures included in the park.

Park Avenue runs down the center of this photo with Central Park and Madison Avenue flanking it on the left. Madison Avenue runs parallel to Central Park on the East Side starting around 57th Street, Madison Avenue offers approximately twenty blocks of unparalleled shopping for haute couture, art, and antiques. On the East Side, Park and Lexington avenues offer a mix of upscale residential dwellings with office space. Helmut Jahn's postmodern buildings have provided some of the most exotic additions to the city's skyline. Two of these are visible here: the pyramid-topped building in the foreground is Park Avenue Tower and the circular pyramid-topped building abutting Lexington Avenue is 750 Lexington Avenue.

The Central Park Zoo at Fifth Avenue and 64th Street is the country's oldest municipal zoo and dates from 1873. Olmstead and Vaux did not want to include a zoo, but the park received so many gifts of animals that they established a menagerie in pens behind the Arsenal building (center back) until a zoo could be built. Eventually, in 1875 the first permanent zoo building was erected. In the 1980s it underwent a $40 million renovation. Exhibits are arranged around three climate zones—Tropic, Temperate, and Polar—with over 450 animals and over 130 species represented.

WOLLMAN MEMORIAL RINK

The Wollman Memorial Rink is located near the Central Park Zoo in the southeast corner of the park at 62nd Street. An ice skating rink in the winter, it provides a venue for rollerbladers in the summer. The recent rebuilding of the rink was financed by Donald Trump.

DELACORTE THEATER AND BELVEDERE CASTLE

The Delacorte Theater in the foreground is home to New York City's beloved Shakespeare in the Park. To the left of the theater is the Great Lawn, which accommodates both picnickers and softball players. On the right is Belvedere Castle, a mixed-use facility that includes a weather station as well as a nature observatory offering exhibits, nature workshops, and educational programs.

The Sheep Meadow's great open lawn on the park's west side, once the site of concerts, has been designated as a quiet zone with kite flying the most vigorous activity allowed. Sunbathing is the favorite low-key activity here. To the left is the lavishly decorated Central Park restaurant, Tavern on the Green, though only its parking lot is visible here.

The Jackie Onassis Reservoir fills most of the East Side of the park and around it is a popular jogging path. The Guggenheim faces the reservoir and is part of "museum mile," a 35-block stretch of museums along Fifth Avenue. The huge complex that has encroached into the park is the Metropolitan Museum of Art. To its left one can see some of the many baseball diamonds within the Great Lawn.

The Macy's Thanksgiving Day Parade starts on the Upper West Side at 77th and Central Park West and takes a route down through Columbus Circle to Broadway, and then proceeds the rest of the way to Macy's. Stretching from 59th to 125th Street, the Upper West Side is bounded by Central Park on the east and the Hudson River on the west.

VIEW OF CENTRAL PARK FROM HARLEM

In this view looking south from Harlem you can see Central Park, the Upper East Side, the Upper West Side, and downtown Manhattan in the distance.

Before it became the official residence of the mayor of New York, the land was the site of a fort. George Washington recognized the strategic value of this parcel of land overlooking Hell's Gate where the East River, Harlem River, and Long Island Sound converge. The fort was destroyed by bombardment by the British and in 1799 Archibald Gracie, a Scottish immigrant, bought the property for a country retreat. Gracie had established a successful trading company and become one of the city's wealthiest residents. The city reacquired the property in 1896 as part of East End Park. In 1942 Robert Moses, parks commissioner, convinced city authorities to make it the official mayor's residence and Fiorello LaGuardia moved in.

The "Met" on Fifth Avenue is among the most popular tourist attractions in the city, with an annual attendance of over 4.5 million. Its first building was erected on this site in 1870; the latest addition was completed in 1990. It is the largest art museum in the Western Hemisphere with over three million works that span world culture from prehistory to the present. J. Pierpont Morgan donated his collection valued at $60 million to the museum in 1913. The permanent collections fill over 220 galleries and include Eastern, Egyptian, European, Greek, Islamic, Medieval, Roman, and 20th Century art.

The Guggenheim Museum, located at 1071 Fifth Avenue at 89th Street, is the only building designed by Frank Lloyd Wright in New York City. Guggenheim, a copper mining magnate, commissioned Wright in 1943 to design a building to exhibit his collection of avant-garde artists. It took over 16 years to complete Wright's complicated and controversial white funnel-shaped structure. The building opened to the public in 1959. The museum has a permanent collection of over 6,000 works from Impressionists to the present day. In the early 1990s the museum underwent a two-year expansion and renovation to refurbish Frank Lloyd Wright's masterpiece and to add a 10-story tower, which provides 31,000 square feet of exhibition, public, and administrative space.

UPPER EAST SIDE

"Museum mile" is a 35-block stretch of Fifth Avenue bordering Central Park and is home to some of the city's most prestigious museums including the Frick, Cooper-Hewitt, Guggenheim, Metropolitan Museum of Art, Whitney Museum of American Art, and American Museum of Natural History.

DAKOTA APARTMENTS

This view from the Dakota's backside shows its trademark steeply-pitched roof covered with dormer windows and its location across from the lake at Central Park West.

When Edward Clark, director of the Singer Sewing Machine Company, decided to build a first-class luxury apartment house it was considered a major speculative gamble. The era's wealthy were unaccustomed to apartment living and the remote location was described as being as far from civilization as the Dakota Territory (the building's address is 1 West 72nd Street at Central Park West). Clark liked this description so much that he named his apartment The Dakota, even carrying the theme to the use of

random Western motifs in the building. With 65 suites ranging from four to 20 rooms, it was the biggest

apartment house in the city when completed. Clark died before he could see that his plan was a success—the building was fully rented prior to its opening and over time developed a long waiting list. The Dakota has been home to the rich and famous ever since. Among its 20th century residents was John Lennon, who brought the building unwelcome notoriety when he was gunned down outside its entrance in 1980.

The Art Moderne Majestic Apartments is one of a select group of landmark apartment buildings facing Central Park West that includes the San Remo, Langham, and Dakota, (seen here to its left). The 31-story Majestic was built shortly after new zoning laws permitted taller residential buildings with setbacks and towers.

Along with the Dakota and Majestic Apartments, the San Remo is a landmark of the Central Park West skyline. Designed by Emery Roth in 1930, the Italian Renaissance-style San Remo was one of the last great apartment buildings constructed before the Depression. The two towers are topped by elaborate structures that are finished with circular temples, which attractively conceal water towers. This feature became one of the architect's signature design elements.

COLUMBUS CIRCLE

Broadway diagonally intersects Eighth Avenue, Central Park West, and Central Park South at Columbus Circle. The name of the circle was changed to its present one after a local Italian businessman spearheaded a fundraising drive to commission a statue commemorating Columbus' discovery of America. A marble statue of Columbus stands atop a 27-foot-high column in the center of the circle. The black glass building in the center is the Trump International Hotel and Tower. To its right is the Maine Monument.

LINCOLN CENTER

Lincoln Center for Performing Arts on Columbus Avenue at 64th Street is considered by many to be the preeminent performing arts center in the United States. Three white marble buildings with flat roofs and colonnades surround the elevated rectangular plaza: the Avery Fisher Music Hall, the Metropolitan Opera House, and the New York State Theater. Founded in 1883, the Metropolitan Opera House is one of the world's great opera companies and stages over 200 performances during its 30-week season. The 14-acre complex also includes, among others, the oldest orchestra in the United States, the New York Philharmonic, the Juilliard School of Music, the New York City Ballet, and the American Ballet Theater.

New York's African-American community is the largest of any American city and has grown due to an influx of West Africans, many of whom have found a home in Harlem. An open-air African Market at 116th and Malcolm X Boulevard (also known as Lenox Avenue) offers leather goods, clothing, jewelry, and curios from throughout West Africa such as batik fabric, colorful hand-woven shirts, and straw hats.

Harlem covers approximately five square miles north of Central Park beginning at 125th Street and extending up to 175th Street. In Harlem, many well-known Manhattan thoroughfares take on new names: Eighth Avenue becomes Frederick Douglass, Seventh Avenue becomes Adam Clayton Powell, and Sixth Avenue becomes Malcolm X Boulevard. In 1658, the Dutch named this area, which was a farming community, Nieuw Haarlem, after a city in Holland. After the Civil War, it grew into a fashionable area of brownstones. Around 1910 rural Southern blacks streamed into central Harlem. In the 1920s, the famous Harlem Renaissance began, which lasted up until the Great Depression. During the Depression the neighborhood went into a long period of decline that lasted until the 1990s. Since then, the area has been experiencing a renaissance as buildings are renovated and new tenants and businesses move in.

The Apollo Theater is located at 253 W. 125th Street in Harlem's commercial district. Constructed in 1914, it initially offered vaudeville and burlesque shows for a middle-class white population. It is more renowned for its role as one of America's preeminent centers for black talent and entertainment. In the 1930s its famous variety show format was instituted, and the Apollo still conducts "Amateur Night at the Apollo" every Wednesday night, just as it has since the 1940s. Among the famous entertainers who have performed here are Billie Holiday, Duke Ellington, Louis Armstrong, Bessie Smith, Gladys Knight, and Bill Cosby.

Riverside Drive begins at West 72nd and extends north past the George Washington Bridge, paralleling the Hudson River. In this section are Grant's Tomb and the neighborhood of Morningside Heights.

Grant's Tomb, overlooking the Hudson River and Riverside Park, is the largest mausoleum in the world. Built as the final resting place for Civil War general and U.S. President Ulysses S. Grant and his wife, their sarcophagi are modeled after Napoleon's tomb. Displays inside cover Grant's achievements during the Civil War and his two terms as president. Inscribed on the building is "Let us have peace," part of a speech Grant made when accepting the nomination for the presidency in 1868.

The Columbia University Campus spreads from 114th to 120th streets and from Broadway to Amsterdam Avenue. It is the lifeblood of the uptown student neighborhood of Morningside Heights.

Situated on a 13-acre site at 1047 Amsterdam Avenue, the Cathedral of St. John the Divine is the seat of the Episcopal Bishop of New York and the world's largest Gothic cathedral. Its vaulted ceiling is as high as a 17-story building and its interior is as large as two football fields and can accommodate 6,000 seated people. Begun in 1892, work stopped for 41 years at the onset of World War II and was not resumed until 1982. The grounds include resident peacocks and the Biblical Garden, planted with trees and flowers that grow in the Holy Land and labeled with references to the biblical passages in which they are mentioned.

Founded in 1754 as King's College, Columbia University is the nation's fifth oldest institution of higher learning. This Ivy League school offers courses in every field of professional endeavor. Dominating this image and the campus is the Italian Renaissance-style domed Low Memorial Library. The Low Memorial Library is the central edifice of the campus, which was designed in form of a Greek cross. The building is no longer actually used as a library and has housed administrative offices since the 30s. Its limestone facade stands in counterpoint to the other brick and stone buildings. To the right is St. Paul's Chapel and in front of the library is Daniel Chester French's sculpture, "Alma Mater," the symbol of this great university.

Begun in 1927 and opened for its first service three years later, Riverside
Church is modeled after Chartres Cathedral. It spans a two-block wide area.
Its 392-foot-high tower is topped by a 74-bell carillon.

Riverbank State Park is a new multi-use complex serving the neighborhood of Harlem. It includes athletic facilities, a wonderful carousel, and spectacular views of the George Washington Bridge.

The George Washington Bridge spans the Hudson River between Manhattan and New Jersey Palisades and is the fourth largest suspension bridge in world. It was designed by Swiss engineer Othmar Amman, who also designed the Verrazano Narrows Bridge, and opened in 1931. At the foot of the bridge is the lighthouse popularized in the 1942 children's classic, *The Little Red Lighthouse and the Great Gray Bridge*.

A view from the George Washington Bridge looking south toward Manhattan.

The Henry Hudson Bridge spans the Harlem River and leads into the affluent Riverdale section of the Bronx. The Henry Hudson Parkway parallels the Hudson River.

Manhattan is an island and requires a lot of bridges, tunnels, and ferries to move commuters and visitors into and out of the city. Shown here are Washington Bridge (Manhattan to the Bronx), the Alexander Hamilton Bridge, and the High Bridge footbridge.

The Grand Concourse, paralleled by railroad tracks on the right, is the main north-south artery of the Bronx. Edgar Allen Poe lived the last three years of his life in a cottage located on the edge of a park at East Kingsbridge Road and Grand Concourse.

Fordham University was founded in 1841 as a Jesuit College. The Gothic fortress-type building in the center is Keating Hall. Edward's Parade quadrangle is in the center of the campus. Behind it lies the New York Botanical Garden, at 200th Street and Southern Boulevard. The domed building is one of 11 glass pavilions that comprise the Enid A. Haupt Conservatory, modeled after the crystal pavilion greenhouses of Kew Gardens in London.

The New York Botanical Garden was founded in 1891 to gather and classify plants worldwide with an emphasis on North and South American specimens. While its horticulture and display of plants are a favorite attraction of New York residents and visitors alike, its primary function is as an internationally renowned plant sciences research center. The 250-acre park includes wetlands, 40 acres of New York City's original forest, ponds, a river and waterfall, and 16 specialty gardens.

Bronx Park is home to both New York Botanical Garden and the Bronx Zoo, opened in 1899. The official name of the Bronx Zoo is the New York Zoological Park and it is ranked among the top world-class zoos. It is the largest urban zoo in America with 265 acres of parklands, woods, and streams. The zoo exhibits over 4,300 animals representing 674 species. A monorail takes visitors on a two-mile journey through the Wild Asia habitat.

Yankee Stadium is the home of the New York Yankees of the American League. The stadium is also know as the house that (Babe) Ruth built and was opened in 1923. It holds over 57,000 people. The Yankees have been World Series champions 25 times.

This is not a single bridge but a 17-mile network of bridges and roads connecting three boroughs: Manhattan, Bronx, and Queens. On the Manhattan side the Triborough Bridge entrance is at E. 125th Street and Harlem River Drive. It was completed in 1936 as an alternative to the Queensboro Bridge for the communities of Bronx, Queens, and Harlem. Hell's Gate Bridge is nearby, which crosses from Astoria to the Bronx with its 1,017 foot parabolic arch and a three-mile concrete viaduct.

QUEENS

Queens, along with Brooklyn, is part of Long Island and is primarily a
residential area.

Located in northwest Queens, closer to Manhattan than JFK International Airport, La Guardia is approximately eight miles northeast of the city and provides quick access to Manhattan via the Triborough Bridge.

Rikers Island has been a city penitentiary since 1935, when the facility on Welfare Island was relocated here. The first facility was the Men's House of Detention. Since then five other correctional facilities have been added. Rikers Island in the East River is joined to Queens by a bridge that is inaccessible to the public. It is named after its 1664 owner, Abraham Rycken. In 1884, New York City annexed the property of about 87 acres. Through landfills, it eventually increased to over 400 acres.

Shea Stadium, home of the NY Mets, was opened in 1964, the same year that the New York World's Fair opened in nearby Flushing Meadows-Corona Park. It also hosted the history-making 1965 Beatles concert and a visit from Pope John Paul II in 1979.

QUEENSBORO BRIDGE

Queensboro Bridge connects eastern Midtown Manhattan with Brooklyn. Transportation was the key factor in the unification of the boroughs and vital ingredients were the Brooklyn, Manhattan, Williamsburg, and Queensboro bridges, along with the subway and electric trolley cars.

Here we see the Williamsburg Bridge, Brooklyn. Brooklyn Heights is in the foreground and the Manhattan and Brooklyn Bridges are in the background.

Brooklyn is the most populous of New York City's boroughs and along with adjoining Queens comprises the western end of Long Island. It is bounded by the East River, Queens, the Atlantic Ocean, and New York Bay. Coney Island is at the southern end of Brooklyn and on the edge of the Atlantic Ocean. Once an upscale seaside resort, today this playground for generations of immigrants and New Yorkers is still popular but has faded into neglect. The first amusement park opened in 1895. When a subway link was established in 1920, a five-cent ride allowed New Yorkers to escape the city's stifling heat to enjoy the beach and amusement park rides.

This photo shows Coney Island's two major amusement parks: Astroland and Deno's Amusement Park. Coney Island's Cyclone roller coaster (in the back) dates from 1927. This famous rickety wooden coaster is 3,200 feet long with speeds of up to 68 miles per hour and nine drops (including one 90 foot-plunge). The Thunderbolt coaster, visible in the foreground, was closed long ago due to safety concerns. The 150-foot tall Ferris wheel with two concentric rings of cars is the Wonder Wheel (1920). The tower in the center is the closed Parachute Jump. The Riegelmann Boardwalk, opened in 1923, runs for four miles along Brooklyn's Barrier Island and was the inspiration for the Coasters' song, "Under the Boardwalk." Tourists can still enjoy hot dogs at Nathan's Finest, salt water taffy, fudge, thrill rides, and the beach, as well as the nearby New York Aquarium.

The Verrazano-Narrows Bridge is the second largest suspension bridge in the world (after England's Humber Bridge) and links Brooklyn and Staten Island at the former guard posts of the Narrows, Fort Hamilton, and Fort Wadsworth, respectively. The bridge is named in honor of Giovanni da Verrazano, the first European explorer to sail into New York harbor. It is sited at the mouth of Upper New York Bay. The New York City Marathon starts on Staten Island and crosses over the bridge and New York Harbor to Bay Ridge, Brooklyn, to continue through all five of the city's boroughs.

One of the best bargains in New York—its free—the Staten Island Ferry offers excellent views of Manhattan and the Statue of Liberty during its one-hour trip between Lower Manhattan and Staten Island. Although discovered in the 16th century by Giovanni da Verrazano, Staten Island remained largely unsettled and rural because of its isolation from the rest of the city. It was only after the ferry began service to the island and the Verrazano-Narrows Bridge was built that the island developed. Inset is the Whitehall Terminal at Whitehall and South streets, Battery Park, and a close-up of the Staten Island Ferry boats.

Lincoln Tunnel provides a vital line between New Jersey and Midtown Manhattan. In the center you can see the toll plaza and behind it the arches of Lincoln Tunnel's three underwater tubes for vehicular traffic. There are a total of 13 lanes. The center tube opened in 1937 followed by the other tubes in 1945 and 1957.

This rarely seen view of the Statue of Liberty provides a good look at the wonderful details of the folds in her copper clothes. The uplifted arm was not installed properly in 1886 and was strengthened when the statue was completely refurbished for her centennial. The torch was also modified to restore its original design; the glass flame lit from within was replaced with a gold-plated copper flame lit with reflected light.

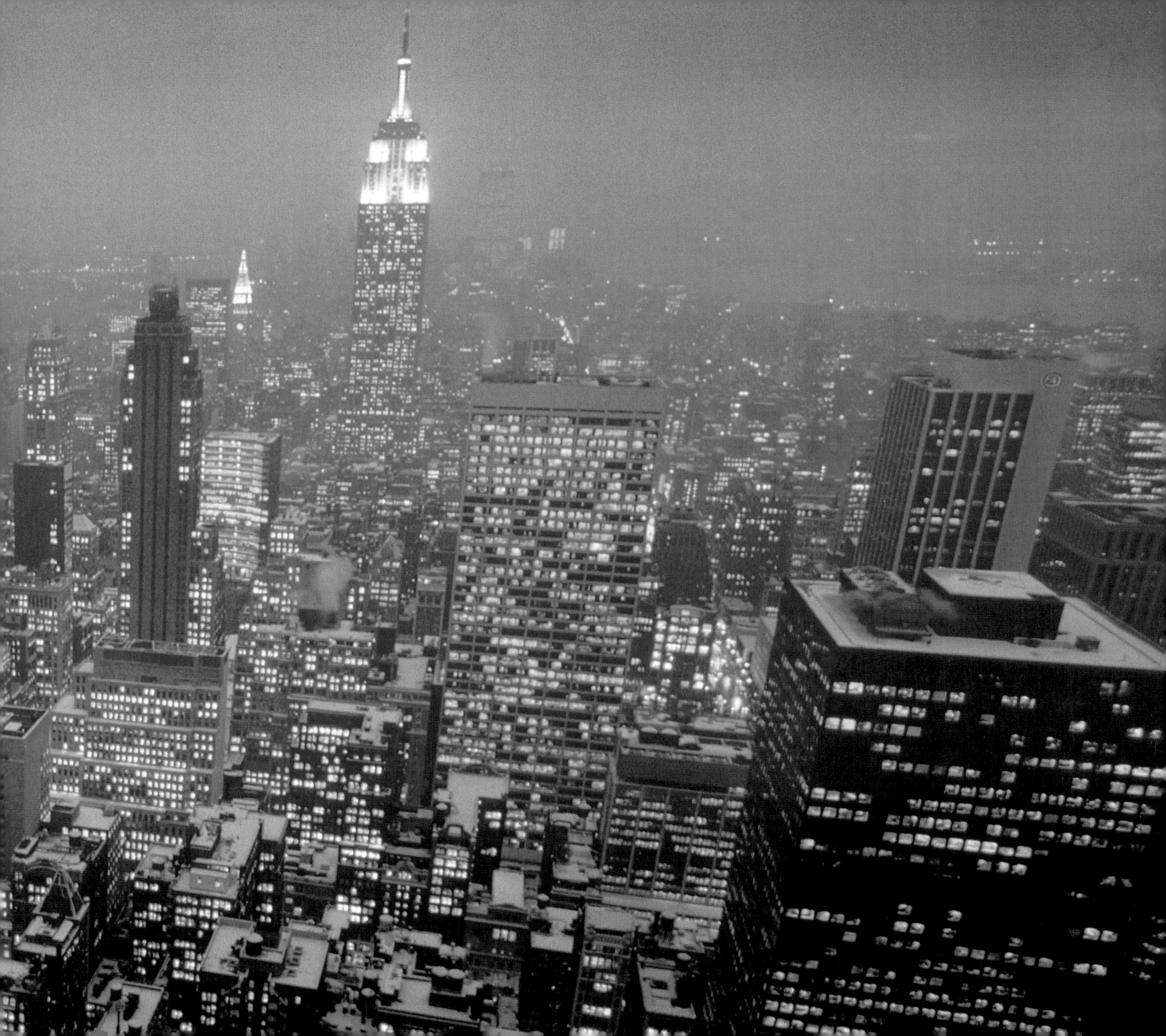

INDEX